Advance Praise

You have to have a great game plan to thrive in the game of life. This includes nutrition, movement, recovery, and most importantly the mindset to create the environment for a lifetime of energy and fulfillment.

—Mark Verstegen, President/Founder Athletes' Performance, Author of *Core Performance* (www.coreperformance.com)

In an easy-to-understand way, sports psychologist Dr. Jim Afremow has illuminated the importance of building "mental muscle." His strategies are useful not only to athletes but to those in other fields—in short, anyone seeking a road map to peak performance.

—Doug Carroll, *Arizona Republic*

Using the performance principles in **Lengthen Your Line**, *Dr. Jim Afremow has helped me reach the top of my game.*

—Grant Irons, *Oakland Raiders*

Dr. Jim Afremow has packaged the perfect combination of practical information, discovery activities, and input from performers in business, sports, science, and the arts. Reading **Lengthen Your Line** *will inspire you to reach a new level of excellence.*

—Jim Brown, PhD, Executive Editor, *Sports Performance Journal*

Dr. Jim Afremow's, **Lengthen Your Line** *is a treasure trove of ideas and inspiration. It combines the science of Western psychology while integrating some essential Eastern wisdom. The result becomes a guidebook of principles and techniques that help readers create a mind-set to control their winning performance.*

—Stephen Lankton, MSW, DAHB, Author of *The Answer Within*
and *Practical Magic*

Dr. Jim Afremow's performance mind-set is a simple yet powerful concept to enhance performance. It is rooted not only in research but also in common sense. It is useful for performers and scholars alike.

—Deborah Feltz, PhD, Chairperson, Department of Kinesiology,
Michigan State University

Lengthen Your Line

Lengthen Your Line

✦

The 5 Cs for Exceptional Performance in the Game of Life

Jim Afremow, PhD

iUniverse, Inc.
New York Lincoln Shanghai

Lengthen Your Line
The 5 Cs for Exceptional Performance in the Game of Life

iUniverse books may be ordered through booksellers or by contacting:

iUniverse
2021 Pine Lake Road, Suite 100
Lincoln, NE 68512
www.iuniverse.com
1-800-Authors (1-800-288-4677)

ISBN-13: 978-0-595-36318-6 (pbk)
ISBN-13: 978-0-595-80756-7 (ebk)
ISBN-10: 0-595-36318-0 (pbk)
ISBN-10: 0-595-80756-9 (ebk)

Printed in the United States of America

To Anne, of course

This is the real secret of life—to be completely engaged with what you are doing in the here and now. And instead of calling it work, realize it is play.

—Alan Watts

Contents

Acknowledgments

Many people have helped me to lengthen my own line in writing this book. First and foremost, I would like to thank the folks at Tignum, the innovative performance institute committed to increasing the performance level of individuals and organizations. Hans-Jurgen "Jogi" Rippel and Scott Peltin contributed much to the outline, content, and development of this book.

Steven Erickson, MD, head team physician, Dean Cummings, MD, Roger McCoy, MD, Deborah Garland, MD, Todd Davis, MD, Amy Jo Overlin, MD, Jared Dunn, MD, Gary Johnson, MS, ATC, Karla Wright, RD, Sandy Smith, AA, Bonnie Doyle, LPN, and the entire sports medicine staff at Arizona State University—I am fortunate to work with and learn from this cutting-edge team of exceptional professionals. I am also blessed to work with so many outstanding coaches and student-athletes. I would also like to acknowledge Lisa Love, Vice President for University Athletics, Don Bocchi, Sr. Associate AD, Sandy Hatfield-Clubb, Sr. Associate AD, Tom Collins, Sr. Associate AD, and Mike Chismar, Associate AD.

Mark Verstegen, president and founder, and his staff of performance specialists at Athletes' Performance—for modeling excellence. Athletes' Performance is the gold standard for athletic performance training. Thank you for inspiring me to be my best and providing the opportunity to work with your world-class athletes.

Stephen Lankton, MSW, executive director, Phoenix Institute of Ericksonian Therapy, Jane deBrown, PsyD, and Jacqueline Dierks, PhD—I am very thankful for the fantastic mentorship you have each provided.

Friends, family members, and colleagues who read parts or all of the manuscript and offered suggestions: Arthur Afremow, Anne Mauricio, PhD, Kim Milbrandt, Todd Clapper, Doug Carroll, Jim Brown, PhD, Paul De Morgan, Ryan and Kim Smith, Sonja Benson, PhD, Julia Russomanno, MC, and Michael Johnson, PhD.

To Todd Clapper, ASU and junior national water polo coach—I always enjoy our conversations about excellence in sport. I also appreciate your sharing with me the story about "putting the river behind you" from *The Art of War,* by Sun Tzu.

To Kim Milbrandt, my "editor"—thanks for sharing your writing skills and helping me put my thoughts to paper. I look forward to reading your first book.

To Anne, my wonderful and multitalented wife—for your unconditional support and the meaning that you have provided to my life.

Introduction:
Lengthen Your Line

The Mirror

There was once a monk who would carry a mirror wherever he went. One day a priest noticed this and thought to himself "This monk must be so preoccupied with the way he looks that he has to carry that mirror all the time. He should not worry about the way he looks on the outside; it's what's inside that counts." So the priest went up to the monk and asked, "Why do you always carry that mirror?" thinking for sure this would prove the monk's vanity. The monk pulled the mirror from his bag and pointed it at the priest. Then he said, "I use it in times of trouble. I look into it and it shows me the source of my problems as well as the solution to my problems."

—Author unknown

INTRODUCTION

If you deliberately plan on being less than you are capable of being, then I warn you that you'll be unhappy for the rest of your life.

—Abraham Maslow

I was inspired to write *Lengthen Your Line* by the exceptional performers that I have had the privilege to meet in my professional life. Through these relationships, I have learned that what separates exceptional performers from other performers is within everyone's reach.

Exceptional performers have a way of thinking, which I refer to in this book as the performance mind-set, that makes them exceptional. Exceptional performance occurs across all life domains—in business, the workplace, on the playing field, in the performing arts, or in any other competitive environment. The performance mind-set is similar in each performance domain.

The purpose of this book is to offer you the opportunity to learn the techniques you need to develop the performance mind-set. Learning these techniques will help you to become an exceptional performer. Are you interested in answering the question, "How great do I want to be?" If you are interested in being the best that you can be in your profession or performance domain, then this book is for you.

In performance psychology there is a saying, "Where the mind goes, the body will follow." The performance mind-set is about possessing outstanding mental skills. The building blocks of the performance mind-set are clarity, confidence, concentration, composure, and commitment—identified as the 5 Cs in this book.

The performance mind-set is based on Western science and Eastern wisdom. Each chapter is preceded by a Zen story relating to one of the 5 Cs. Philosopher Alan Watts liked to recount that he once gave a book of Zen stories to a friend who was sick. When the friend recovered, Dr. Watts asked him what he thought about the book. The friend said that he did not understand it but that, after reading it, he felt much better.

What does it mean to lengthen your line? Through my work, I have realized that performers can have a preoccupation with their competition. This preoccupation is limiting and prevents them from becoming their best. When I notice this preoccupation in one of my clients, I share with them the following Zen riddle. I draw a chalk line on the floor and ask them how to make the line shorter without erasing its edges. The answer—draw a longer line next to it, thus making the original line shorter in comparison.

The lesson is to make your own line longer (and stronger) rather than to worry too much or to try to cut down the competition (the original line). Be your own yardstick. Focus on chasing your own potential and learning how great you can be in your life and performance domain. The best way to lengthen your line is to perfect your performance mind-set.

1

The Performance Mind-set

The Centipede

A centipede was happy quite,
Until a frog in fun
Said, "Pray, which leg comes after which?"
This raised her mind to such a pitch,
She lay distracted in the ditch
Considering how to run.

—Author unknown

CHAPTER 1

All the world's a stage,
And all the men and women merely players;
They have their exits and their entrances,
And one man in his time plays many parts.

—William Shakespeare

The performance mind-set is the greatest state of mind and emotion for consistent high-level functioning under all conditions. We need this mind-set to be exceptional in everything we do, whether closing a business deal, delivering a speech, or playing in the big game. What are the characteristics or attributes of the performance mind-set? What does it take mentally to be really great in business, the performing arts, sports, and life?

In this chapter, we will begin with experiential activities to explore what your performance mind-set is and what it takes to be exceptional. The next step is to learn how to use the performance mind-set for everyday challenges, in high-pressure situations, and for dealing with life changes. The chapter concludes with what motivates the exceptional performer.

Experiential Activity #1:

Develop a list of mental attributes (e.g., confidence) that you perceive as important to great performance in business, the performing arts, sports, and other fields. Note how the mental attributes identified across these performance domains are similar. Next, list people in your life and top performers in business, the performing arts, sports, and other fields whom you admire. Specifically, list their characteristics that you admire most. Then list examples of times when you have shown these characteristics. I suggest finding a partner for this activity, with whom you can share your list of mental attributes and names.

The performers that you identified most likely have, or had, big dreams (clarity of vision) and a burning desire to achieve them (motivation). They are also confident, focused, composed, and committed. The lesson of this activity is that the same mental attributes are needed for exceptional performance irrespective of whether one is an executive, artist, or athlete. In other words, exceptional performance is exceptional performance.

Experiential Activity #2:

Close your eyes and recall a time in your professional or personal life when you did something exceptionally well and exercised the mental attributes necessary for exceptional performance. This could be a work situation, such as giving a presentation, or perhaps a personal experience, such as playing a game of golf or tennis. Visualize yourself in that moment and recreate that experience in your mind. Identify which attributes were central to making this experience great. Notice where you placed your attention and whether you found your focus narrowing or expanding. Did you feel your performance flowed easily or required great thought? Now recall a time when you were engaged in the same activity but were dissatisfied with your performance. How did your mental state differ between the two performances? Were you less confident? Less focused? Did you lose composure?

We have considered what it takes, mentally, to be successful. There are many commonalities among high achievers and across performance domains. Great performers have an abundance of clarity, confidence, concentration, composure, and commitment. This is the performance mind-set. In the experiential activity above, we also identified that you had a time when you fully experienced the performance mind-set.

There is a misconception that real talent is something you have or do not have and that only some (champions) can be truly great performers. The reality is that everyone possesses the key attributes for exceptional performance. The 5 Cs are learnable, teachable behaviors.

However, the 5 Cs are like mental muscles that must be exercised, in the same way that physical muscles must be exercised. How do you build mental muscle and get in the performance mind-set more often, making excellence the norm? The program outlined in this book, based on the principles of performance and sport psychology, will help you further develop these muscles and release your real talent.

Sport psychology gives me an advantage over myself that no physical training can ever provide. Sport psychology allows athletes to use all of their mental strengths. This gives them a huge advantage over their opponents, as usually their biggest opponent is themselves.

—Ian Thorpe, Olympic gold medalist, swimming

Sport psychologists Terry Orlick and John Partington determined that mental readiness, as rated by 235 Canadian Olympic athletes who participated in the 1984 Olympic games in Sarajevo and Los Angeles, is the most important factor of the three readiness factors (mental, physical, and technical). Many of the interviewed Olympians indicated that they could have reached the top of their game much sooner had they worked on strengthening their mental skills earlier in their careers. An article in the *San Francisco Chronicle* reported, "Olympians demanded more couch time after the 1998 Nagano games. When asked what would help them compete better, most Nagano athletes said sport psychology."

Imagine having the ability to attain the performance mind-set and be exceptional on a regular basis. Imagine how good it would feel going to work or practice each day knowing that the ability to access this mind-set is readily available. Imagine how much more productive and enjoyable your experiences would be.

The Performance Mind-set for the Game of Life

When I am in my painting, I'm not aware of what I'm doing.

—Jackson Pollock

Do you embrace the challenge of the day, whatever it might be? Regardless of performance domain, our day is spent either in or out of the performance mind-set. When we are not in the performance mind-set, we are in an unchallenged state of mind. When we are in the performance mind-set, we are in a state of mind that accepts challenge.

Exceptional performers continually seek ways to lengthen their line by creating and accepting challenges, rather than trying to avoid them. When you are in the unchallenged state of mind you are limiting your ability to perform exceptionally. In a state of mind that accepts challenge the performer is fearless, energized, self-confident, focused, and in control.

How do you know if you are in the unchallenged mind-set? Check in with your emotions or feelings about what you are doing. If you are bored or dreading what you are doing, you are not in the performance mind-set but in the unchallenged mind-set. Examples of the unchallenged mind-set include:

- The professional looking at the clock while in a business meeting
- The athlete going through the motions during a practice drill
- The would-be lawyer procrastinating on preparing for the bar exam
- The violinist showing up to rehearsal with a sense of obligation
- The assembly-line worker goofing-off when the supervisor is not present

Once you notice that you are out of the performance mind-set, simply create a challenge for yourself. A challenge is the best route to the performance mind-set. Discover ways to increase your motivation for what you are doing by (1) making it fun, (2) making it interesting, or (3) turning it into a competition. Be creative! The philosophy here is "challenge your limits, don't limit your challenges."

Begin to identify tasks as challenges or ways to compete against yourself. Tell yourself, "This is exactly what I want to be doing right this moment." When you make life a game, this is the game of life. How fast can I do this? How well can I do this? How much can I accomplish? When you ask yourself these questions, your productivity will increase. When you are fully engaged in what you are doing, your enjoyment increases as well.

A surgeon interviewed on National Public Radio described the same surgery he performs every day. Rather than looking at this as a grim duty, he explained how he challenges himself. Instead of complaining about the lack of variety, he approaches each surgery as an opportunity to perfect his craft. As a result, he enjoys what he does each day.

The Performance Mind-set under Pressure

They throw the ball, I hit it. They hit the ball, I catch it.

—Willie Mays

Do you thrive in high-pressure situations or do you perform poorly? In contrast to the increased motivation needed for everyday tasks, performing under pressure requires a different mind-set. First, you need to develop the necessary skills for your performance. This is accomplished by emphasizing what I call the *practice mind-set*, which involves being analytical, judgmental, and effortful. When you have a practice mentality, you are in a thinking phase.

Second, we need to trust our ability to execute these skills once we learn them. This is accomplished through what I call the *performance mind-set* under pressure, which involves being simple, instinctive, and playful. The performance mind-set is about getting out of our own way and "letting it happen" when it is time to perform. In other words, "train it and trust it." When you have a performance mentality, you are in an action phase.

For example, when learning how to drive a car you are in the practice mind-set, because you must first pay attention to the specific skills that you need to develop. However, once you have learned these skills well, you need to be able to go into the performance mind-set when a high-pressure situation arises, such as taking a driving test. In the high-pressure situation of taking your driving test, paying too much attention to specific skills can impede the proper execution of driving the car. This example illustrates the distinction between the practice and performance mind-sets.

Research shows that we have a tendency to think too much about what we are doing when faced with a high-pressure situation. Specifically, during situations when we are being evaluated and have high expectations of ourselves, we attempt to analyze every aspect of our performance (self-presentation) because we believe that doing so will help our performance.

Dr. Debbie Crews, assistant research professor of exercise science and physical education at Arizona State University, conducted research on why people "choke" under pressure. Dr. Crews used electrodes to measure the brainwaves of subjects in the experiment. She found that one key to success is getting the left and right hemispheres of the brain in balance. While the left hemisphere is the verbal side, the right hemisphere is the creative side (see Table). To achieve a state of balance, the left hemisphere must quiet while the right hemisphere increases activity.

When performing with left-hemispheric dominance in high-pressure situations, you are consistent with the performance psychology maxims "paralysis by analysis" and "if you over-think you will under-perform." This mode of performance often hinders, rather than helps, our performance. In contrast, in non-evaluative performance situations, we focus on doing the task rather than analyzing the step-by-step components of our performance. In this balanced mode of performance, we expend less energy evaluating our performance, allowing ourselves to expend more energy on actually performing. As Yogi Berra said, "How can you hit and think at the same time?"

Table

The Practice Mind-set (Left hemisphere)	The Performance Mind-set (Right hemisphere)
• Active Mind	• Quiet Mind
• Careful	• Playful
• Effortful	• Trusting
• Judgmental	• Accepting
• Analytical	• Creative
• Tendency to complicate	• Tendency to simplify

Gary Kasparov is a chess grandmaster and one of the best chess players in history. After defeating all of his main rivals, he had epic matches with IBM's Deep Blue Supercomputer. Recently, he has given numerous presentations using chess to model business strategy and the importance of keeping a psychological edge in any field. Kasparov has stated that, inevitably, intellect or logic must be replaced by "playing with your gut" in order to perform your best "at the very toughest moments."

How can you trust your training when you are under pressure? The paradox is that you need to be yourself and let your performance happen rather than trying too hard to live up to the moment. There is a Zen saying, "The task is simple, and the student is complicated." Many people try to make their task too complicated, especially under pressure. It is all right to be simple!

This approach is counterintuitive for the ego-driven performer who is preoccupied with self-presentation and the end result. He may ask, "What if I fail?" or "How do I compare?" As a master performer, ask yourself the right questions before you perform. "How much fun can I have?" "What is my aim (target or objective)?" "What do I have to do right now?" Change your questions to change your performance.

Trying: When an archer is shooting for enjoyment, he has all his skill. When he shoots for a brass buckle, he gets nervous. When he shoots for a prize of gold, he begins to see two targets.

—Chuang Tzu

When the Boston Red Sox won the 2004 World Series, eighty-six years of prayers from their diehard fans were answered, and people all over the world cheered. How were the Red Sox finally able to break "the Curse"? Pitcher Derek Lowe stated, "We had fun. We tried to be kids, as much as we possibly could, and it worked." Outfielder Manny Ramirez said, "We don't think out there. We go and play the game the way it is, and that's what it's all about. When you play so relaxed, a lot of things can happen for you."

Trust the instinct to the end, though you can render no reason.

—Ralph Waldo Emerson

Dr. John Eliot, sport psychology lecturer in the department of kinesiology at Rice University, uses the squirrel as a metaphor to illustrate the importance of trusting ourselves in high-pressure situations. Specifically, Dr. Eliot suggests tapping into your "inner squirrel" to perform up to your potential in crunch time. We have all watched squirrels run across high telephone wires with agility and fearlessness. Have you ever wondered how this can be done?

Because the squirrel does not have the capacity to over-think its performance, it operates without fearing that it will fall. Basically, it trusts its training (i.e., looking and doing). This is the performance mind-set under pressure. If we were put in a similar situation, such as walking across a ledge, our brains might lead us to over-think and under-perform.

Experiential Activity #3:

Imagine that you were asked to walk the length of a two-by-four board on the floor. Then imagine that the board is suspended 10 or 20 meters in the air and that you again are required to walk the length of the board. Although the actual required task is identical, would you actually be willing to attempt to walk the length of the board while it is suspended at this height? In your performance domain, what is the equivalent? Is it meeting with the board of directors? Is it taking the game-winning shot? Is it taking your final exam?

In the first step of the exercise, you probably would not pay as much attention to how your knee is bending or how your foot is landing on the board. However, while walking on the board while it is suspended, you evaluate behaviors that are normally automatic because you believe that this evaluation will prevent you from falling. In fact, it is precisely this evaluation that will likely make you fall. Not paying attention to required automatic behaviors assists your performance of a task, while giving attention to automatic behaviors interferes with your performance. The same is true in all performance domains. When being evaluated or when under pressure, self-analysis of performance behaviors that are automatic in your day-to-day work will lead to failure, not success.

To summarize, when you find yourself in a high-pressure situation, keep it simple, be instinctive, and take a playful approach. Do not try to out-perform yourself—be yourself. Avoid the tendency to be overly serious. Follow the KISS Performance Principle: Keep It Super Simple!

Be a Master of Change

Be like water, my friend.

—Bruce Lee

Do you welcome change or do you flounder in the face of uncertainty and ambiguity? The performance mind-set requires tremendous flexibility in a constantly changing world. The "survival of the fittest" principle can be applied to the performance mind-set: you must be willing and able to adapt, or you risk extinction in your performance domain. Bruce Lee compared adaptation to the formlessness of water. When you pour water into a cup, the water takes on the shape of the cup. When you pour water into a vase it takes on the shape of the vase. Flow with change, rather than breaking apart.

It used to be common for a person to work for the same company and live in the same house all of his life. Now the business world requires one to shift and adapt with changing markets, often requiring relocation. Likewise, professional athletes often played on the same team for their entire careers. This is now the exception, and not the rule. As such, these athletes are frequently traded and must continually deal with new teammates and coaches, as well as different living and performance environments. What are the recent or upcoming changes in your life?

When confronted with major change, avoid dwelling on the wrong questions ("Why me?" "Why now?"). Instead, ask the right questions ("How can I benefit?"). Be curious! Above all, be proactive (thriver mode) rather than reactive (victim mode). An exceptional performer in the thriver mode does not just cope with change, they grow from it. When people are in the victim mode they are more likely to be passive and non-receptive to change. As the saying goes, "The best way to predict the future is to create it."

Becoming a Mastery Performer

I need to chase myself and not chase anybody. I've got a big enough tail to chase. I don't need to worry about anybody else.

—Davis Love III

Exceptional performers have high levels of intrinsic and extrinsic motivation. People who are intrinsically motivated perform to be their best. Extrinsic motivation, on the other hand, is doing something for external reasons (money, status, awards). Exceptional performers want to be their best *and* want to win.

Tiger Woods expressed, "It would be nice to win as many majors as Jack [Nicklaus] did. That would be great. But I keep telling you [reporters] this: I want to be a better player at the end of the year than I was at the beginning. If I keep doing that year after year after year, at the end I'll have had a pretty good career." Tiger Woods also stated, "Second place sucks." These quotes illustrate Tiger's emphasis on both intrinsic and extrinsic motivation for playing the game of golf.

The prime motivation for exceptional performers is intrinsic motivation; this is being a mastery performer. Being a mastery performer is about building your performance up and being motivated to do better. These persons are mastery performers because they are continually striving to lengthen their line and reach their own potential. These persons also take pride in being competent in what they are doing and feel worthy of that.

Although extrinsic motivation is critical for exceptional performance, research has also shown us that people who are primarily extrinsically motivated are more likely to burnout. When you are motivated by results and you do not obtain them, you are more likely to give up on your performance. When you are solely motivated by extrinsic reasons, go back to your roots and rediscover what led you to pursue what it is you are doing. Remember, while extrinsic motivation does have significance in positive performance, it is intrinsic—not extrinsic—motivation that is the key to exceptional performance.

Similar to extrinsic motivation, an ego orientation involves demonstrating ability by judging one's performance against others. With an ego orientation, there is an over-emphasis on social comparison. The ego performer is preoccupied with being superior to others, rather than chasing her own potential. Paradoxically, by chasing your own potential and removing ego from performance, you will develop superior ability.

It goes without saying that as soon as one cherishes the thought of winning the contest or displaying one's skill in technique, swordsmanship is doomed.

—Takano Shigeyoshi

Why do exceptional performers continue when they have nothing left to prove? Why do they delay retirement? When exceptional performers are intrinsically motivated they do not have to prove anything, rather they want to keep doing what they love to do. Warren Buffett, one of the richest and most successful businessmen in the world, described himself as "tap-dancing to work every day." Bill Gates continues to lead Microsoft, even though he is the richest person in the world. Exceptional performers know that how one performs relative to one's self is most important. Instead of counting the days until retirement, count the ways you can improve your performance.

Renowned coach Anson Dorrance told soccer great Mia Hamm early in her career, "The vision of a champion is someone bent over, drenched in sweat, to a point of exhaustion, when no one else is watching." Here are three more examples of how exceptional performers apply a mastery orientation to their performance:

- "I paint for myself. I don't know how to do anything else, anyway. Also, I have to earn my living, and occupy myself."—Francis Bacon

- "To race as fast as I can, race by race, one by one, is my only goal. My biggest goal is to just keep improving with each race."—Herman Maier, world-champion skier and two-time Olympic medalist.

- "What I know is, is that if you do work that you love, and the work fulfills you, the rest will come."—Oprah Winfrey

Experiential Activity #4:

Identify your personal motivation. Determine the real reasons why you perform. Why are you in your particular performance domain? What do you enjoy most about it? What makes you passionate about it? How high is your current level of motivation? What keeps you coming back to it?

The first part of this chapter highlighted the importance of the performance mind-set used by the exceptional performer for successfully conquering everyday responsibilities (be creative), high-pressure situations (be simple), and life changes (be curious). The exceptional performer is a mastery performer because they are motivated intrinsically, always trying to perfect their performance.

The following chapters will focus on the 5 Cs of the performance mind-set. With these tools you will be able to gain a better understanding of how you can further develop the performance mind-set. However, before moving on to the 5 Cs, you will need to build a mind gym, which involves the use of mental imagery or visualization to enhance performance. The first section of the following chapter will walk you through steps you can take to build your own mind gym.

Self-reflection:
How great do I want to be?

Step-by-step review of developing the performance mind-set:

Step 1—

Be creative when making everyday situations into challenges

Step 2—

Be simple in high-pressure situations

Step 3—

Be curious when faced with life changes

2

Mental Imagery: Building Your Own Mind Gym

A picture is worth a thousand words.

—Chinese saying

CHAPTER 2

Imagination is more important than knowledge.

—Albert Einstein

Everything that you can imagine is real.

—Pablo Picasso

Mental imagery, also labeled visualization or mental rehearsal, is the process of imagining yourself performing well. Essentially, imagery is preparing for your performances in your head. This is accomplished by creating or recreating experiences in the mind. Imagery rehearsal can be likened to playing a video game: the more you play, the better you will become at the actual task.

Scores of experimental studies have been reported in the scientific literature exploring the effects of mental imagery on physical performance. Drs. Deborah Feltz and Dan Landers, prominent researchers in sport psychology, completed a thorough review of mental practice literature and confirmed the benefits of using imagery for performance enhancement. Their findings demonstrated that imagery is one of the most powerful performance tools that we have in our mental toolbox. Imagery is much more than daydreaming. As with physical practice, imagery requires focus and discipline to reap the full benefit.

Although imagery will not guarantee success in the boardroom or on the playing field, mastery of this tool will increase the likelihood of success. Specifically, imagery works to enhance our performance by perfecting the "mental blueprint" and strengthening the "muscle memory" for the task at hand. Imagery is used by virtually all Olympic athletes as a crucial part of their training program. In fact, imagery can be used to mentally prepare for all performances, whether attempting a bench press or making a presentation.

The brain does not perceive much of a difference between real and imagined experiences. Consider nightmares, for instance, people who have nightmares of being chased. Although the experience is not real, they eventually awaken frightened and unnerved, often having the exact same physical sensations (increases in heart rate and respiration) as if they in fact had been chased.

Experiential activity #5:

Close your eyes and hold your arms straight out in front of yourself. Turn one hand palm up and the other palm down. Now, imagine balancing a bowling ball (or heavy object) in the hand with the palm up. Feel the full weight of the ball forcing your arm toward the ground. Then, imagine that there is a helium balloon tied to the wrist with the palm down. Feel the balloon tugging and lifting this hand. Open your eyes and observe that the one hand has dropped and other hand has elevated as if this imagined experience actually happened. Try this activity with some of your friends.

How can you best use imagery to enhance your performance and develop the 5 Cs? The first step is to design a personal mind gym or mental training studio in your imagination. Build the room to your specifications and include all of the resources that you might possibly need, such as any equipment, books, or tapes related to your field. Include a comfortable chair in your mind gym, in front of a wide-screen high-definition TV with a DVD player for your imagery rehearsal. Perhaps you can even sketch your plans on paper to make the room more "real." The mind gym can be likened to a virtual-reality simulator used by NASA to prepare astronauts for space missions.

The second step is to spend 10–20 minutes each day or every other day in your mind gym developing your exceptional performance skills. Make sure that your environment has few distractions. Find time in the morning or evening, or perhaps during any downtime, to visit your mind gym. Imagine yourself walking into the room and sitting down in front of your high-definition TV. What you choose to imagine during each particular training session will depend on what you want to accomplish. Realize that the more regular and structured your practice, the more vivid and controllable your mental images will become. Involve all of your body's senses. Imagery rehearsal should always be as much about "feelization" ("feeling" the performance) as it is about "visualization" ("seeing" the performance).

Let us begin with your first mind gym exercise—exceptional performance. Each of the 5 Cs will include a mind gym script pertaining to the addressed topic. You may want to read each script several times before completing the exercise. Also, experiment with playing background music to set the tone. Consider making personal audiotapes or CDs of these imagery scripts or perhaps developing your own scripts.

Mind Gym #1: Exceptional Performance

Get into a comfortable position with your neck and back well-supported. Have a sense of pride as you sit or lie down. Close your eyes and turn your attention to your breathing. Inhale slowly, deeply, and effortlessly through your nose. Exhale slowly, fully, and effortlessly through your mouth. Let all the muscles, from your head to your toes, relax and go limp as you exhale. Feel all of the tension leave your body. Images are often clearer and more effective when you are relaxed. In this tranquil state, your imagination will flow and you will be safe and free to produce the desired images. Continue to breathe deeply in this manner for a few minutes.

Remember a time when you had a great performance. Now begin to recreate your scenario. Involve all of your senses (see it, feel it, hear it, taste it, smell it). Notice as many details as possible. View yourself from the perspective of a spectator, as if you were witnessing this performance as it is unfolding. Now switch the perspective so that you are in your body, viewing the performance through your own eyes. Make it feel as if you are performing it right now.

Now let go of that performance and imagine that you are in your mind gym that you have specially built to develop your exceptional performance skills. Imagine that you have available all of the resources you need. These resources could be physical items like books or tapes, or anything else that you could possibly need. Now imagine that you are seated on a special chair in your mind gym and you have a wide-screen high-definition TV with a DVD player. On a table is a DVD of your ideal performance and you now put it into the player and press play on the remote control. Imagine that you are a spectator watching your own powerful performance—everything is falling into place as you perform. Again, make it as if you are executing the performance right now. Now imagine on the bottom of the screen there are subtitles, like you would see while watching a foreign film. Imagine that, as these subtitles appear on the bottom of the screen, they are capturing your thoughts and feelings. Note the positive words and powerful emotions. You are totally focused. You are projecting confidence. Let yourself fully experience this image and enjoy watching and feeling yourself perform to the best of your abilities. Then, step into that scene and become the performance.

Spend several minutes experiencing yourself performing incredibly well at your chosen task. When finished, slowly begin to open your eyes, sit quietly for a few minutes, and then orient yourself to your surroundings.

Self-reflection:
If I can't "see it" or "feel it," how can I achieve it?

Step-by-step review of developing mental imagery skills:

Step 1—

Image what you want to happen in your performance

Step 2—

Use all of your senses

Step 3—

Mentally practice when you have downtime

3

Clarity

Destiny

During a momentous battle, a Japanese general decided to attack even though his army was greatly outnumbered. He was confident his men would win, but they were filled with doubt. On the way to the battle, they stopped at a religious shrine. After praying with the men, the general took out a coin and said, "I shall now toss this coin. If it is heads, we shall win. If tails, we shall lose. Destiny will now reveal itself."

He threw the coin into the air and all watched intently as it landed. It was heads. The soldiers were so overjoyed and filled with confidence that they vigorously attacked the enemy and were victorious. After the battle, a lieutenant remarked to the general, "No one can change destiny." "Quite right," the general replied as he showed the lieutenant the coin, which had heads on both sides.

—Author unknown

CHAPTER 3

Tell me, what is it you plan to do with your one wild and precious life?

—Mary Oliver

When I finally realized what I wanted in life that is when my life changed.

—Dan O'Brien

Irrespective of choice, everyone leaves a mark or legacy by which they will be remembered. Each person has a choice regarding whether that mark will have a meaningful impact. Clarity is defining what that mark is and how it will bring purpose and meaning to your life. Clarity is also knowing your personal and professional dreams. As C.S. Lewis stated, "You are never too old to set another goal or to dream a new dream."

In relation to the performance mind-set, clarity is how you get to where you want to go. The performance mind-set is how you put it to use. Dreams are often confused with goals. Dreams create the feeling you get from the connection of who you are and what you do. Goals are the outcomes (such as a pay raise). When you set a dream you feel more vibrant. Vincent Van Gogh stated, "The only time I feel alive is when I'm painting."

In this chapter we will introduce three anecdotes, describing real-life stories of clarity in the performance mind-set. The next step is identifying and breaking through your psychological barriers. This chapter will conclude with an opportunity for self-reflection and an imagery exercise that will help you use your imagination to gain greater clarity in your life.

> *I ain't jogging…I'm running seven-minute miles. I'm definitely putting my foot to the pedal these next few years…I don't want to look back and say I cheated myself. There were some guys who had a shot at three hundred victories, but let themselves go and never got there. I ain't playing this game for the paycheck every fifteen days or to watch the paint dry. I ain't doing this for the money. I want to leave my mark on the game.*
>
> —Roger Clemens

There is a saying, "If you don't enjoy the journey, then you probably won't enjoy the destination." The dream is about enjoying the journey. The reward for having dreams is that you are inspired rather than required to accomplish more goals. The goal is a by-product of your mission. The purpose of goals in relation to commitment will be discussed in another section.

Here are three anecdotes illustrating the power of dreams:

- Ernest Shackleton, a veteran explorer at the turn of the 20th century, attempted the first cross-continental journey of Antarctica. To obtain a crew, he used the following advertisement:

  Notice: Men wanted for hazardous journey. Bitter cold. Small wages. Long months of complete darkness. Constant danger. Safe return doubtful. Honour and recognition in case of success.

  Thousands of men responded to the advertisement and wanted to go on the expedition. Given the danger, why did so many men want to join Shackleton? The reason is that they were inspired by Shackleton's dream, and the advertisement offered them a dream of their own. The endeavor that followed has become legendary and inspired productions of numerous books and movies.

- Milton Erickson was an eminent psychiatrist who worked with a depressed wealthy widow from Milwaukee, Wisconsin in the 1950s. The woman was very lonely and kept herself isolated, except for attending church services. While visiting Milwaukee, Dr. Erickson was asked to meet with her at her home. The depressive tone in the house was noticeable, except for some African Violets that the woman had planted herself. Rather than acknowledging the depressive tone, Erickson focused on the beautiful flowers. He commented that he experienced the woman as selfish because she had a gift in growing African Violets and she was not sharing this gift with other people. The intent of Erickson's intervention was not to upset the woman but to encourage her to consider how she was living her life and "plant a seed" for how she could be living it differently. Years later, Erickson received a copy of her obituary in the mail, which indicated that a large number of people attended the funeral of the "African Violet Queen." Erickson learned that his meeting with the woman years earlier resulted in her setting a dream of becoming more connected with others by gifting them her beloved African Violets at ceremonious times in their lives, such as weddings and birthdays. As a by-product, her loneliness and depression diminished. Through this dream, she became well-known and beloved by her community.

- Phil Knight is the co-founder of Nike and a former University of Oregon track star. While working on his MBA, Knight completed a project which involved devising a small business. In 1968, he teamed up with his former coach, Bill Bowerman, to produce high-quality running shoes. Their first shoes had soles made on Bowerman's waffle iron and were sold out of the trunk of Knight's car. Once Knight had clarity about his business plan, he was off and running. Knight stated, "We wanted Nike to be the world's best sports and fitness company. Once you say that, you have a focus. You don't end up making wing tips or sponsoring the next Rolling Stones world tour." Under Knight's leadership, Nike completely changed the fitness culture and the Oregon-based company has become a $12 billion business.

Bucky's Experiment

In 1927, R. Buckminster Fuller ("Bucky"), 32, stood on a bridge near Lake Michigan. He planned to commit suicide by leaping into the freezing waters. He was disheartened after losing his child, and many of his business and scientific ideas had been discredited. Rather than take the jump, Bucky had a 'eureka' moment and self-reflected: Do I not belong to the universe? What could I do for the good of humanity? He decided to devote his "new" life to asking himself, "What is it on this planet that needs to be done that probably won't happen unless I do it?" He called this quest of what an average man could accomplish "an experiment." Today, R. Buckminster Fuller is acknowledged in the scientific community for the invention of the geodesic dome, among many other notable achievements.

Experiential Activity #6:

Identify a dream worth pursuing in your career, such as developing a novel approach to your line of business that could make a difference in your life as well as in others.' What is your equivalent to growing African Violets and sharing them with others? Think ahead to the end of your career. Project yourself several years in the future to your retirement party or banquet. What would you want others to say about you when your career is over? How about when your life is over? Dreams are not confined by limitations or what we may think is realistic. Dreams can be inspired by life events that make us smile or traumatic life events that make us frown.

For example, John Walsh, now the host of "America's Most Wanted," began his career as a partner in a hotel management company. In 1981, his 6-year-old son, Adam, was abducted and later found murdered. Mr. Walsh's traumatic life event motivated him to eventually create a national television show that would help bring criminals to justice. The show has been extremely successful and Mr. Walsh was recently named as one of "100 Americans Who Changed History" by CBS.

Break through Psychological Barriers

Imagine the possibility of unlimited possibilities.

—Unknown

In order to be exceptional, you must eliminate your psychological barriers. When you consider an aspect of your performance to be unrealistic or impossible then you have discovered a psychological barrier. A classic example of a psychological barrier was the four-minute mile in track and field. At one time, there was a common perception that running a mile in less that four minutes was physically impossible. On May 6, 1954, Roger Bannister, a 25-year-old medical student, ran the mile in 3:59.4. He recalled, "Doctors and scientists said that breaking the four-minute mile was impossible, that one would die in the attempt. Thus, when I got up from the track after collapsing at the finish line, I figured I was dead." Bannister's record lasted only 46 days. Once the psychological barrier had finally been removed, 16 other runners had managed the feat within 18 months of the famous breakthrough. What can you identify as the four-minute mile in your life?

Mind Gym #2: Clarity

Begin by closing your eyes and turning your attention to your breathing. Take some slow, deep breaths. Feel all of the tension leaving your body. Continue to breathe deeply in this manner for a few minutes.

Imagine that you have entered your mind gym. Now that you have identified a dream for your life, consider how your life will be different. In living this dream, your life would become instantaneously more exceptional, as if you experienced a breakthrough. What observable indicators suggest that this breakthrough had occurred? If you had a DVD of your life six months prior to and six months after experiencing a positive "breakthrough," what would you see and hear on the segment of DVD six months after the breakthrough that would inform you that your personal and professional life was more exceptional? In brainstorming the answer to this question, consider all changes, whether big or small. However, it is important that the post-breakthrough changes are specific and observable behaviors. For example, are you more engaged in meetings (e.g., asking questions, offering feedback)? Are you exercising more frequently? Are you spending more time with your spouse and children? Are you smiling more often? What healthier foods are you eating? Consider all the things that you would want to observe on the 6-month segment of the DVD following your breakthrough.

On the table is a DVD labeled, "Personal Breakthrough." Put this new video in the player and watch all the positive changes you are making in your life. Then, step inside that scene and into the image, looking at your performance through your own eyes. Make it feel as if you are performing it right now. Notice where your eyes look. Notice how your body moves. Spend several minutes experiencing your dream. When finished, slowly begin to open your eyes, sit quietly for a few minutes, and then orient yourself to your surroundings.

Recognize that you have the power to incorporate these changes into your daily life immediately. As you incorporate these changes, others will notice that there has been a shift, informing you that you are on the path to being more exceptional.

Self-reflection:
If I don't have a dream, how am I going to have a dream come true?

Step-by-step review of developing clarity:

Step 1—

Set a dream

Step 2—

Use your dream for inspiration

Step 3—

Make it happen

4

Confidence

The Tea Master

A Samurai and a Master of the Tea Ceremony happened to meet. The meeting did not go well, and they began to argue. The Samurai challenged the Tea Ceremony master to a duel to the death with swords, and said: "Meet me here today at 4 o'clock in the afternoon, and we shall fight."

Honor would not permit the Tea Ceremony master to refuse the challenge, so he had to agree. But he was frightened, and went to his own teacher of Tea Ceremony, to ask him what to do. "I have never held a sword in my hand in my life," he said. "He will surely kill me."

The older Tea Ceremony master replied with a calm smile. "Do not worry," he said. "Go meet him at the appointed time, and do what you know how to do. Perform the Tea Ceremony."

At four o'clock, the Samurai arrived with swords. But the Tea Ceremony master arrived with charcoal, matches, a tea kettle, water, cups, and began to prepare the tea. The Samurai watched in awe. Finally, when the tea was ready, the Tea Ceremony master handed a cup to the Samurai.

The Samurai sipped the tea properly. When he finished, he said to the Tea Ceremony master: "I am defeated. You have united body and soul so perfectly, you defeated me.'

—Author unknown

CHAPTER 4

There is no such thing as over-confidence.

—Bob Rotella

If you have no confidence in self, you are twice defeated in the race of life. With confidence, you have won even before you have started.

—Marcus Garvey

Confidence is knowing that you can do what you set out to do. Confidence is also about having a positive view of yourself as a performer and as a person. Remember, "You can't outperform your self-image." Having a positive view of yourself is not the elimination of all doubt. Self-confident performers believe in themselves irrespective of doubt, as they do not accept doubts as an accurate reflection of their abilities.

In regard to the performance mind-set, there is often a "which comes first?" or "chicken and egg" dilemma. Mediocre performers believe success produces confidence and they cannot be confident until they are successful. Exceptional performers know that confidence precedes success and have faith in their abilities independent of results.

In this chapter, we will introduce how confident performers think, feel, and act. The next step is to incorporate high levels of confidence into your performance. The chapter concludes with a self-reflection question and a mental imagery exercise that will help you use your imagination to strengthen your performance confidence.

Marie Curie, awarded the 1911 Nobel Prize in chemistry, understood the value of confidence in her own performance. She stated, "Life is not easy for any of us. But what of that? We must have perseverance and above all confidence in ourselves. We must believe that we are gifted for something and that this thing must be attained." She knew she needed confidence in order to succeed in a male-dominated field, especially in the era in which she lived.

This is an example of how the power of confidence will affect your performance. When you have confidence in your performance you are able to transcend others' expectations. Developing and maintaining confidence is absolutely necessary to being in the performance mind-set.

Dr. Albert Bandura, Stanford psychologist, has pioneered research on the effects of self-efficacy (a construct akin to confidence) on performance. People who exhibit high levels of self-efficacy think, feel, and act differently than people with low levels of self-efficacy in the performance mind-set. According to Dr. Bandura, self-efficacy influences:

- The decisions we make
- How much effort we expend
- How we feel
- Whether we take an active role in our life

How can you incorporate high-level confidence into your performance? Here are some techniques for helping you increase your confidence. Choose the techniques that will work for you.

Choose to think confidently—Instead of entertaining ideas to perform poorly, give yourself reasons to perform well. Highly confident performers use affirmations such as, "My best is the best" and "I can do this." Less confident performers have thoughts such as, "I can't" and "I am awful."

During the 1970s Tom Weiskopf was one of the top golfers in the world. In spite of his success, Jack Nicklaus often derailed him in his quest to win major championships. Weiskopf attributed his short-comings to a lack of confidence against his rival. Reflecting upon his career, Weiskopf stated, "Jack knew he was going to beat you. You knew Jack was going to beat you. And Jack knew that you knew that he was going to beat you."

Choose to feel confidently—Highly confident performers remember the sights, sounds, and feelings associated with their best-ever performances. Less confident performers dwell on the feelings associated with their worst performances. Briefly putting yourself back in your magic moments will help you get in the best state of mind and emotion to meet the challenge of the business at hand.

Choose to act confidently—Model your favorite performers in your chosen field in how they present themselves. Highly confident performers radiate confidence and always look like they are doing well regardless of their performance. They keep their facial expressions and body language upbeat. Less confident performers exude defeat by dragging their feet with pained facial expressions. William James, the father of American psychology, stated, "Act the part, and you will become the part."

Experiential activity #7:

Slump your shoulders, lower your head, and frown. While in this posture, try to feel happy. Now, look up in the air, raise your arms, and smile. While in this position, try to feel sad. This experiment demonstrates the importance of our body language in affecting our mood and our performance.

Recall your highlights—Think back to all of your biggest achievements in your performance domain. Recall successfully attaining desired goals. Highly confident performers have a long-term memory for their successes and a short-term memory for failures. Less confident performers have a long-term memory for their failures and a short-term memory for their successes.

Acknowledge positive feedback—Take into account praise from admired or trusted persons in your life. Remember all of the wonderful things family members, coaches, friends, instructors, teachers, and others have said about your performance and your potential.

Experiential activity #8:

Make a list of your high points and highlights in your performance domain. Record the accomplishments that have made you proud. Include positive feedback from important people throughout your life. Refer to this list when your confidence is at a low level.

Be thoroughly prepared—One of the principal ways that you can build and sustain your confidence is to set the stage for success and then to go out there and let it happen. Arthur Ashe stated, "One important key to success is self-confidence. An important key to self-confidence is preparation." Highly confident performers consider all of their hard work as building a machine that will be tough to beat. Less confident performers do not expect to do well and so fail to prepare themselves accordingly.

Be appropriately assertive—Give yourself permission to perform your best and to succeed without feeling guilty. Highly confident performers do what is necessary to win without worrying about their competitors' feelings. They are also direct and honest in their communication with others. Less confident performers feel like they do not deserve to win and are overly concerned with their competitors' feelings. They are also unduly passive and indirect in their communication. As such, they often feel resentment and frustration for not getting what they want.

Have a scorer's mentality—People differ on how they respond to success versus failure while performing. Highly confident performers expect success to last and failure to turn around. They maintain faith and "keep shooting." Babe Ruth expressed the scorer's mentality when he declared, "Every strike brings me closer to the next home run." Less confident performers expect a good start to be short-lived and a poor start to persist.

Win the confidence competition—Turn confidence into a competition. Highly confident performers separate themselves form less confident performers by competing against their self-doubt rather than succumbing to it. In an interview with Johnny Miller, Angelo Argea, Jack Nicklaus's caddie, was asked to explain why he did not read greens or help with club selection. "He asked me to do two things," Argea replied. "When he's not playing well, one, remind him that he's the best golfer out there. And, two, that there are plenty of holes left."

Mind Gym #3: Confidence

Begin by closing your eyes and turning your attention to your breathing. Take some slow, deep breaths. Feel all of the tension leaving your body. Continue to breathe deeply in this manner for a few minutes.

Imagine that you have entered your mind gym. You are ready to increase your confidence. On the table is a DVD labeled, "Confidence." Now put this DVD into the player. As you press play, notice that the video begins with a recent performance in which your confidence was low and your performance suffered. The video is in black and white. Notice the subtitles at the bottom of the screen. What are your negative thoughts and emotions? How is your body language?

Rewind the performance. This time you are totally confident. Your performance is now in color. Make the image brighter, turn up the volume, and bring the scene closer. Watch the same performance the way you wanted it to happen. Notice the subtitles at the bottom of the screen. What are your positive thoughts and emotions? How is your body language?

Now select an upcoming performance. Create your ideal scenario. Involve all of your senses (see it, feel it, hear it, taste it, smell it). Notice as many details as pos-

sible. View yourself from the perspective of the performer, so that you are in your body and viewing the performance through your own eyes. Make it feel as if you are performing it right now. All of the confidence techniques are at your disposal. Spend several minutes performing with pure confidence. You are decisive, clear, and having fun. Any mistakes or errors are just flukes and you quickly rebound.

You may also wish to view a mentor completing your performance. The mentor can be a real person in your life, a mythical or historical figure (such as Buddha, a warrior, or an athlete), or someone you create in your imagination that has the characteristics you admire most. Watch the mentor flawlessly perform your task and then wave you in as a replacement. Your mentor has full belief in your abilities.

Spend several minutes experiencing your exceptional performance. When finished, slowly begin to open your eyes, sit quietly for a few minutes, and then orient yourself to your surroundings.

Self-reflection:
Do I have a can-do attitude?

Step-by-step review of developing confidence:

Step 1—

Think confidently

Step 2—

Feel confidently

Step 3—

Act confidently

5

Concentration

The Present Moment

A Japanese warrior was captured by his enemies and thrown into prison. That night he was unable to sleep because he feared that the next day he would be interrogated, tortured, and executed. Then the words of his Zen master came to him, "Tomorrow is not real. It is an illusion. The only reality is now." Heeding these words, the warrior became peaceful and fell asleep.

—Author unknown

CHAPTER 5

Concentrate all your thoughts upon the work at hand. The sun's rays do not burn until brought to a focus.

—Alexander Graham Bell

The time is now. The place is here.

—Dan Millman

Concentration is the ability to focus on the business at hand and refocus quickly when distracted. The purpose is to become totally absorbed so that anything unnecessary to your performance fades to the background. Think of how absorbed a child is playing with a new toy. Concentration is necessary for the performer's skills to be effectively employed. High quality focus is energy concentrated like a laser beam. Low quality focus is energy scattered like light from a light bulb. When all of your energy is aimed at your objective it is more powerful than if it were dispersed.

In the performance mind-set, it is important to recognize when you are overwhelmed and to be able to shift your focus. When you notice that you have become overwhelmed by the big picture of your performance, switch your focus to the small picture. When you notice that you have become mired in the details of your performance, switch your focus to the big picture.

In this chapter, we will introduce how focused performers perform in present time and quickly refocus when distracted. The chapter concludes with a self-reflection question and a mental imagery exercise that will help you use your imagination to improve your performance concentration.

Perform in Present Time

Learn from the past, prepare for the future, and perform in the present.

—Gary Mack

Have you ever had difficulties shifting from one performance domain to another? Many people think of one area of their life while performing in another area of their life. When an athlete puts on their uniform they can think of this as becoming the player and leaving any personal issues behind. This is why it is important to develop a mental locker. Using a mental locker is a metaphor for allowing yourself to switch roles. This process will help you to use the performance mind-set for the appropriate role.

Experiential Activity #9:

Draw your own mental locker with the number of shelves corresponding to the number of areas of your life. For instance, a business professional might have four shelves (personal, social, family, work). Then, draw an object or symbol on each shelf that represents these areas of your life (CD of favorite band or personal hobby, spouse or family members, paycheck or sales award). Now that you have created your own mental locker, when transitioning from one role to another, remain on one shelf by not worrying about the other areas of your life. Make sure that whatever you are doing you are doing to the fullest.

Most exceptional performers have developed an individualized pre-performance routine that helps to get them in the performance mind-set. When you have had your best performances or most successful work days, what were some of things that you did to get in the mind-set that set you up for a good performance? Did you arrive early? Did you meditate or visualize success beforehand? Did you eat a healthy breakfast?

Now, think about your worst performances. What did you do differently on these days? Understanding differences between behaviors prior to your best and worst performances will help you further refine your personal routine and perform your best more consistently.

Your pre-performance routine should be consistent with who you are as a person. For instance, some people like to be off by themselves and not talk to anyone, while others prefer to joke around and be more social. The objective is to be engaged and fully focused when it is time to perform or start your day. How you get there requires an individual approach.

The 4 Ps of Concentration

There are 4 Ps or general recommendations for sharpening your concentration. Personalize each P so that it fits well with your performance. The first P is to remain positive rather than negative while you are performing. The second P is to perform in present time rather than focus on the past or the future. While performing, do not make it a history lesson! Rather, keep moving forward. The third P is to focus on proper execution rather than what you hope to avoid. The fourth P is to focus on the process rather than the product or end result. Do not write the review until the performance is over! Work the process and the results will take care of themselves. Following are some examples illustrating the 4 Ps of concentration.

- *Positive*—In baseball a player should recognize that, while his team is behind, there are plenty of innings left.

- *Present*—In business an executive needs to focus on the current business deal, rather than on a past or future business deal.

- *Proper*—In the performing arts a musician should focus on giving her best performance, rather than trying to avoid making mistakes.

- *Process*—In school a student should focus on answering each question on the test to the best of her ability, rather than worrying about her grade.

A common misconception is that we can block-out distractions. This is equivalent to telling someone not to think about a pink elephant. The more you try not to think about the elephant, the more you think about the elephant. Instead of trying to block-out distractions, focus on your target. Block-in, don't block-out.

It is also important to consider the physical side of concentration. If you find yourself running out of steam it will be that much harder to concentrate. As such, it is important to rest well, eat healthy, and get in better shape. Having a strong connection between the mind and the body is essential to your performance.

Refocus When Distracted

Work is hard. Distractions are plentiful. And time is short.

—Adam Hochschild

Throughout our daily lives it is impossible to remain focused on what we are doing at all times. Exceptional performers have developed the ability to refocus quickly in the face of distractions. It is not a matter of eliminating distractions, but about gaining the tools to deal with them. You do not have to be a victim to your distractions.

In the performance mind-set it is important to be able to manage distractions. Exceptional performers are able to identify the distractions that affect their performance. Distractions can be either internal or external. To increase your self-awareness, ask yourself these two questions: What are my major distractions while I perform? Are they internal or external?

Internal Distractions

- Pain or fatigue
- Negative thoughts/images
- Destructive emotions
- Personal concerns
- The past/future
- Mistakes/errors
- Thirst/hunger

External Distractions

- Noise or unexpected sounds
- Spectators/observers
- Teammates/colleagues
- Coaches/bosses
- Weather conditions
- The environment
- The clock/scoreboard

Here are some techniques for helping you to refocus when distracted. Choose the techniques that will work for you.

Practice good eye control—Distractions are only distractions if you identify them as distractions. If you notice that you are caught up in looking at irrelevant external stimuli that is interfering with your performance, look away.

Have a refocusing spot—When you are distracted find a landmark in your environment at which you can look to regroup. This could be something on your desk or on the wall that you can utilize for refocusing.

Control your environment—Identify ways to reduce distractions and clutter in your performance environment. An executive or student might close her door, turn off her phone, or clear her desk.

Take a deep breath—When you notice that you are becoming internally distracted, take a cleansing breath. A few slow, deep breaths will help you to quiet your mind.

Put on a rubber band—Some people find it helpful to wear a rubber band around one of their wrists. When they identify that they are distracted or in a negative frame of mind in a performance situation, they gently snap the band to help them to refocus. Snap back!

Use a key phrase—Develop a phrase or motto that will help you to quickly refocus once you have become aware that you are distracted. Some actors are taught to tell themselves, "I'm back." Once you realize that you are out of focus, you can go back in focus. Popular phrases following a mistake or error include, "So what? Keep going," "Let it go," "Next step," "Turn the page," and "Forget it and focus."

Mind Gym #4: Concentration

Begin by closing your eyes and turning your attention to your breathing. Take some slow, deep breaths. Feel all of the tension leaving your body. Continue to breathe deeply in this manner for a few minutes.

Imagine that you have entered your mind gym. You are ready to increase your concentration. On the table is a DVD labeled, "Concentration." Now put this DVD into the player. As you press play, notice that the video begins with a recent performance in which you lost your focus and your performance suffered. Perhaps there was a long break in the competition or there was taunting by an opponent. The video is in black and white. Where is your focus? What are your distractions (internal, external)?

Rewind the performance. This time you are totally focused. Your performance is now in color. Make the image brighter, turn up the volume, and bring the scene closer. Watch the same performance the way you wanted it to happen. You can notice that your focus has narrowed and any distractions outside of your vision fall away.

Now select an upcoming performance. Create your ideal scenario. Involve all of your senses (see it, feel it, hear it, taste it, smell it). Notice as many details as possible. View yourself from the perspective of the performer, so that you are in your body and viewing the performance through your own eyes. Make it feel as if you are performing it right now. All of the concentration techniques are at your dis-

posal. Spend several minutes performing with pure focus. You are locked into the task at hand. Any distractions are trivial and you quickly refocus.

You may also wish to view your mentor completing your performance. Watch the mentor flawlessly perform your task and then wave you in as a replacement. Your mentor has full belief in your abilities.

Spend several minutes experiencing your exceptional performance. When finished, slowly begin to open your eyes, sit quietly for a few minutes, and then orient yourself to your surroundings.

Self-reflection:
Am I focused or scattered?

Step-by-step review of developing concentration:

Step 1—

Perform in present time

Step 2—

Make it routine

Step 3—

Snap back when distracted

6

Composure

Self-Control

One day there was an earthquake that shook the entire Zen temple. Parts of it even collapsed. Many of the monks were terrified. When the earthquake stopped the teacher said, "Now you have had the opportunity to see how a Zen man behaves in a crisis situation. You may have noticed that I did not panic. I was quite aware of what was happening and what to do. I led you all to the kitchen, the strongest part of the temple. It was a good decision, because you see we have all survived without any injuries. However, despite my self-control and composure, I did feel a little bit tense—which you may have deduced from the fact that I drank a large glass of water, something I never do under ordinary circumstances."

One of the monks smiled, but didn't say anything.

"What are you laughing at?" asked the teacher.

"That wasn't water," the monk replied, "It was a large glass of soy sauce."

—Author unknown

CHAPTER 6

Nothing gives one person so much advantage over another as to remain always cool and unruffled under all circumstances.

—Thomas Jefferson

Always keep your composure. You can't score from the penalty box; and to win, you have to score.

—Horace

Composure is the ability to maintain emotional control in performance situations. There are four basic emotions that can influence your performance. These are glad, sad, mad, and bad. Feeling glad refers to having fun in the moment. Feeling sad refers to being down and depressed. Feeling mad refers to being angry and frustrated. Feeling bad is when we experience guilt or anxiety.

In the performance mind-set, emotions are not necessarily good or bad; rather it is the appropriateness of an emotion that affects how we perform. For instance, the level of how glad you feel can affect your performance in many different ways. If you are over-excited or under-excited you will not perform at your best. To remain in the performance mind-set, it is important to find a balance between the extremities of these emotions. A problem exists when an emotion persists for a much longer time or with a greater intensity than it normally would.

In this chapter, we will introduce how exceptional performers control fear, sadness, and anger. The chapter concludes with a self-reflection question and a mental imagery exercise that will help you use your imagination to increase your composure.

Excitement (glad) and fear (bad) produce similar physiological responses. However, excitement is based on a positive appraisal of the situation whereas fear is based on a negative appraisal of the situation. Follow the guidelines for fear in also dealing with over-excitement:

Fear: Get Your Butterflies to Fly in Formation

Fear is only as deep as the mind allows.

—Japanese proverb

Fear is the response to feeling threatened in a harmful situation. Fear provoking emotions generate the "flight instinct." The "flight instinct" is a physiological response with the goal of removing ourselves from the situation. Physiological responses include blood rushing to the major muscles and increased alertness.

Here are some techniques for effectively dealing with fear in performance situations:

- **Be the predator, not the prey**—Attack the challenge head-on as opposed to running from it (offensive versus defensive mind-set).

- **Pace, don't race**—Keep a consistent speed when performing, as we tend to rush when anxious.

- **Downplay the importance**—Maintain perspective by realizing that what you are doing is important but not overly important.

- **Act "as if"**—It is okay to be nervous, but you do not have to perform as if you were nervous.

- **Embrace the rush**—Use the adrenaline as extra energy for an exceptional performance.

- **Breathe deep**—Be mindful of your breathing, as our breathing often becomes shallow or rapid when anxious.

- **Smile** ☺

Sadness: Rebound from Disappointment

Many of life's failures are people who did not realize how close they were to success when they gave up.

—Thomas Edison

Sadness is the response to feeling defeated or rejected. There can also be a sense of deep loss or unmet expectations when there is a failure to reach an objective. According to Basketball Hall of Fame coach John Wooden, "Bad times can make you bitter or better." People who are sad or depressed have a negative view of themselves and their performance situation and are pessimistic about their future.

Exceptional performers realize that failure is never fatal and that mistakes are an important part of the learning process. John Wooden referred to mistakes as "the building blocks of success." Warren Buffett stated, "Wrong decisions are a part of life. Being able to make them work out anyway is one of the abilities of those who are successful."

Dan Gable won 181 consecutive wrestling matches in high school and college and then coached the University of Iowa wrestling team to 15 national championships. He stated, "Every great athlete has fallen short at some point. Great athletes become great because they refuse to let their setbacks derail them from their determined quest to be the best."

Here are some techniques for effectively dealing with sadness in performance situations:

- **Feel the pain**—Discuss your thoughts and express your feelings with family and friends, rather than ignoring such feelings.

- **Team up**—Get help and support from important people in your personal life and performance domain.

- **Learn the lesson**—Determine as best you can the root cause of what happened (technical, tactical, or mental) and make positive corrections.

- **Have unconditional self-acceptance**—Rate your performance behaviors, not your worth as a person (separate self-esteem from performance-esteem).

- **Cope, don't crumble**—Search for ways to become stronger and better from difficult experiences.

- **Maintain a sense of pride**—Take on the attitude that you are really good at bouncing back from setbacks.

- **Smile** ☺

Anger: Use It; Don't Abuse It

The angry man will defeat himself in battle as well as in life.

—Samurai maxim

Anger is the response to feeling trespassed on or helpless about a situation. Anger-provoking emotions generate the "fight instinct." The "fight instinct" is a physiological response with the goal of protecting ourselves or removing an obstacle in a situation. Physiological responses include blood rushing to the hands and arms and an increased energy level.

Here are some techniques for effectively dealing with anger in performance situations:

- **Act like a pro**—Be professional by taking responsibility for your actions in every situation.

- **Have a physical release**—Clench your hands into a fist for a few seconds then open your hands and let go of all the anger.

- **Channel the anger**—Anger can be likened to electricity: you can either electrocute yourself or light up your performance.

- **Stop the spiral**—When anger has gotten the best of you, distract yourself or temporarily remove yourself from the situation.

- **Have a sense of humor**—Learn to laugh off mistakes and to not take disappointments too seriously.

- **Think "cool" thoughts ("No big deal.")**—Stop rehearsing angry thoughts ("I can't stand this!") as they will increase your anger level.

- **Smile** ☺

Experiential Activity #10:

Identify situations in your performance domain in which you were overly "glad," "sad," "bad," or "mad" and your performance suffered as a result. Which of the above techniques would be most helpful the next time you are in a similar situation?

Turn Positive Thoughts into Positive Performances

Thought is the sculptor who can create the person you want to be.

—Henry David Thoreau

What you think affects how you feel, and how you feel affects how you perform. Self-talk is what we say to ourselves throughout the day as we meet each challenge. While performing, keep your self-talk task-oriented and focused on what you are doing. Our self-talk can be productive, neutral, or unproductive. Productive thinking stems from self-talk that assists us in performing as well as we can.

Thought replacement is an excellent technique to change our thoughts from a negative to a positive channel. Thought replacement is a three-step process:

1.   Notice the unproductive thought as it occurs ("Here we go again")

2.   Stop the unproductive thought (think "No!" or "Stop!")

3.   Replace the unproductive thought with a productive thought ("I'll do great on the next call").

Realize that too much self-talk ("inner chatter") can be counterproductive. Keep your thoughts simple and positive throughout the day as you meet obstacles, make decisions, and resolve problems. Remember, "You get more of what you think about."

Experiential Activity #11:

This exercise will help you to become more self-aware of your current thinking habits. Take 20 paper clips and put them in your front pocket. Every time you have an unproductive thought about yourself or your performance ("I don't want to do this"), take a paper clip from your front pocket and transfer it to your back pocket. Keep track of how long it takes to empty your front pocket. The longer it takes the more productive your self-talk.

The Circle of Excellence

We cannot choose our external circumstances, but we can always choose how we respond to them.

—Epictetus

In order to be fully in the performance mind-set, we must use our energy on that which is within our control. Realize that we only have control of ourselves. External factors are beyond our control. Keep in mind that we can always choose how we respond to the things beyond our control to maximize our performance. This realization provides you with the freedom necessary to be in the performance mind-set. With this freedom you are able to have greater emotional control. Following are examples illustrating factors that you can and cannot control.

Can Control

- Attitude
- Effort
- Strategy
- Diet
- Routines
- Communication

Can't Control

- Audience
- Competitors
- Performance conditions
- Teammates/colleagues
- Referees/judges
- Family/friends

To increase your self-awareness, identify the most important factors about your performance.

1. Draw a circle on a sheet of paper.

2. Ask, "What can I control?" (Place inside the circle).

3. Ask, "What is beyond my control?" (Place outside the circle).

What can you influence that is outside your circle (outcomes)? What do you need to accept (weather)? You can be more influential with people (outside the circle) by improving your communication (inside the circle). You can try to make the best of difficult circumstances rather than flying off the handle.

For example, we cannot control traffic delays on the way to work in the morning (outside the circle), but we can control whether we let it negatively affect the rest of our day by resolving to leave for work earlier in the mornings (inside the circle). Excellence is about using our energy to "control the controllables" by staying "inside the circle."

"Houston, We've Had a Problem"

On April 11, 1970, Apollo 13 was to be the third mission to land on the moon. However, an explosion in one of the oxygen tanks caused the spacecraft to lose electricity, water, and a dangerous amount of oxygen. Following the accident, astronaut Jim Lovell radioed to mission control, "Okay, Houston, we've had a problem here." Although this phrase was understated it was not meant to underestimate the significance of the situation. The astronauts and mission control were able to manage their emotions, and regarded their situation as a problem to be solved. Gene Kranz, the flight controller, declared that "failure is not an option." As a result of their teamwork and emotional control, the astronauts' lives were saved.

Mind Gym #5: Composure

Begin by closing your eyes and turning your attention to your breathing. Take some slow, deep breaths. Feel all of the tension leaving your body. Continue to breathe deeply in this manner for a few minutes.

Imagine that you have entered your mind gym. You are ready to increase your composure. On the table is a DVD labeled, "Composure." Now put this DVD into the player. As you press play, notice that the video begins with a recent performance in which you lost your composure and your performance suffered. Perhaps you got angry and lost your cool, or perhaps your anxiety level was too high.

The video is in black and white. Notice the subtitles at the bottom of the screen. What are your negative thoughts and emotions? How is your body language?

Rewind the performance. This time you are totally composed. Your performance is now in color. Make the image brighter, turn up the volume, and bring the scene closer. Watch the same performance the way you wanted it to happen. Notice the subtitles at the bottom of the screen. What are your positive thoughts and emotions? How is your body language?

Now select an upcoming performance. Create your ideal scenario. Involve all of your senses (see it, feel it, hear it, taste it, smell it). Notice as many details as possible. View yourself from the perspective of the performer, so that you are in your body and viewing the performance through your own eyes. Make it feel as if you are performing it right now. All of the composure techniques are at your disposal. Visualize dissipating future "bad," "mad," or "sad" emotions using these techniques. Spend several minutes performing with absolute composure. You are poised and your intensity level is steady.

You may also wish to view your mentor completing your performance. Watch the mentor flawlessly perform your task and then wave you in as a replacement. Your mentor has full belief in your abilities.

Spend several minutes experiencing your exceptional performance. When finished, slowly begin to open your eyes, sit quietly for a few minutes, and then orient yourself to your surroundings.

Self-reflection:
Am I pumped or panicked?

Step-by-step review of developing composure:

Step 1—

> Fear: Get your butterflies to fly in formation

Step 2—

> Sadness: Rebound from disappointment

Step 3—

> Anger: Use it; don't abuse it

7

Commitment

Chasing Two Rabbits

A martial arts student approached his teacher with a question. "I'd like to improve my knowledge of the martial arts. In addition to learning from you, I'd like to study with another teacher in order to learn another style. What do you think of this idea?" "The hunter who chases two rabbits," answered the master, "catches neither one."

—Author unknown

CHAPTER 7

The main thing is to keep the main thing the main thing.

—Stephen R. Covey

All the trophies and all the championships in the world don't change the fact that today I have to practice.

—Tiger Woods

Commitment is about honesty and action with respect to your dreams. Are you willing to take the necessary steps to follow through with your commitment and live your dreams? If not, you are being dishonest with yourself about making a real commitment. What needs to change for you to perform your best? What do you need to start doing? What do you need to stop doing? The higher your level of commitment, the more exceptional you will be in your performance domain.

In the performance mind-set, it is important to remember that you are your own boss. In order to succeed, you must make an active choice to commit to your dreams. Each day is an opportunity to strengthen your mind-set and improve your performance. This commitment will raise your performance stock. Inc. yourself!

In this chapter, we will introduce how exceptional performers develop real commitment. The chapter concludes with a self-reflection question and a mental imagery exercise that will help you use your imagination to increase your commitment.

Inc. Yourself

People are notorious for making New Year's resolutions on which they never follow through. Research has shown that at least a six-month commitment is often necessary to make exercise and similar behaviors a habit in our lives. Why do our good intentions to make positive changes sometimes go bad? Often, there is an unrecognized part of us that is in conflict with our intentions.

Imagine that you have two CEOs housed in your head. One CEO is more driven and the other CEO is more carefree. The driven CEO makes a lot of "should" statements ("I should exercise more regularly," "I should eat healthy foods," "I should put more hours in at the office."). If you are too driven you risk burning out. In contrast, the carefree CEO makes a lot of "wish" statements ("I wish that exercise wasn't so hard," "I wish that I could eat whatever I wanted," "I wish that I could go on a long vacation."). Although both sides appear to have competing interests, they are really two sides of the same coin.

Specifically, each side has the best interests of the company in mind. The driven CEO is about the bottom-line and increasing profit. The carefree CEO is about making sure that the human needs are met and trying to avoid burnout. Often, the two CEOs are engaged in a power struggle, resulting in the company losing. A winning company requires that both CEOs work together as a team and that they dialogue about effective change. This occurs when the coin is balanced (or spinning) rather than resting on one side.

The first step in working toward sustainable change is to be aware of these two parts of ourselves and to acknowledge and validate both of them. The second step is to work toward integration so that each CEO has equal shares in the company.

Experiential Activity #12:

Using this metaphor of two CEOs housed in your head, identify a time when the two CEOs were in conflict. What was the conflict? What was the driven CEO saying? What was the carefree CEO saying? What was the result? If the conflict was not resolved successfully and the outcome left you feeling unexceptional, how can you negotiate between the two CEOs more effectively next time?

For example, you had planned to stop at the gym on your way home from work. The driven CEO is telling you that you should go to the gym, while the carefree CEO is telling you to go pick up a pizza and rent a movie. How do you negotiate these two competing desires? If you really need a mental and physical break to recover from a long day at the office, actively chose to pick up the movie and perhaps something healthier to eat. However, if the carefree CEO's voice is motivated by avoiding your commitment to exercise, stop at the gym.

Make Time for Regeneration

Sometimes the most urgent thing you can possibly do is take a complete rest.

—Ashleigh Brilliant

It is important to make an equal commitment to work hard and rest well. Regeneration helps you "recharge" for improved health and performance. You need to be able to shut down before you can restart. Exceptional performers do not allow excuses to get in the way of their regeneration. They understand that they cannot wobble between their commitments, when they are working they work and when they are resting they rest.

If you think you do not have time for regeneration, prove it! Record what you do each day and indicate when you are "on" and when you are "off." During your "off" periods, if you are thinking about your performance then you are not making a real commitment to regeneration. When you come home at the end of the day "punch out"; you are no longer on the clock.

Regeneration is about quality not quantity when it comes to rest and relaxation. It is also not about the amount of hours you sleep per night, but about how deeply you sleep. Consider all the ways, new and old, that help you to "recharge."

- Watch a movie
- Listen to music
- Read a magazine
- Walk in nature
- Yoga and meditation
- Meet with a friend
- Exercise
- Take a power nap

Daily Goals

Every single day I wake up and commit myself to becoming a better player.

—Mia Hamm

In order to maintain a real commitment, it is important to set daily goals. Every morning, ask yourself, "What can I do today to be exceptional?" List three to five specific behaviors that you want to accomplish. Listing three to five behaviors will help you to find your focus for accomplishing what is most important. This may include personal as well as professional goals. At the end of the day, ask yourself honestly, "Was I exceptional today?" Setting these goals will help you to stay on track for an active role in your commitment. Remember that, if you experience a setback, you are only one day away from being back on track.

Set three mental game goals prior to important or high-pressure performances. Too many goals will defeat the purpose of this technique. Make sure that these goals are within your control. For example, a musician might use this technique prior to a concert as follows:

To play my best, I will:

1.   Follow my pre-performance routine

2.   Trust my talent

3.   Play one note at a time

Your daily goals and mental game goals can be written on an index card and placed in your back pocket for a positive reminder throughout your day or before or during your performance.

Get out of the Bucket

Keep away from people who try to belittle your ambitions. Small people always do that, but the really great make you feel that you, too, can become great.

—Mark Twain

Motivational speaker Les Brown uses the metaphor about a bucket of crabs to teach us about the power of socialization. When you are carrying a bucket of crabs you do not need a lid to keep them inside. The reason why you do not need a lid is because if one crab tries to get out the others try to pull it back in. The same principle can be applied to our lives. The more we attempt to become exceptional the more people attempt to bring us down, sometimes unintentionally. People often feel uncomfortable when left behind with either jealousy or concern.

Experiential Activity #13:

Draw a circle and inside of the circle write the names of the people in your life who are supportive. Then, outside of the circle, write the names of the people in your life who are "crabs." Give yourself permission to be appropriately assertive with the people you identified as being outside of the circle and limit their negative influence in your life.

Turn Adversity into an Adventure

This is the Chinese symbol for "crisis." It is a combination of the symbols
for "danger" and "opportunity."

If you dream big you will be faced with big obstacles. This requires that you have a full, complete commitment. When we are faced the inevitable obstacles we can choose whether to view them as adversity or turn them into an adventure.

When we turn these obstacles into an adventure we utilize all of our resources to accomplish more and this makes us stronger.

Erik Weihenmayer lost his eyesight at age 13 due to a rare hereditary disease of the retina. Although he was faced with this disability, he was able accept it and has since thrived. He is an accomplished rock climber and in 2001 became the first blind person to summit Mt. Everest. He said, "We are always going to face adversity, life is not meant to be easy." Weihenmayer has been able to accept his disability and make the most of his opportunities.

Experiential Activity #14:

On a separate sheet of paper, use the three column technique below to develop a list of 10 or more typical situations in your life and performance domain. Determine the adversity response (past behavior) and the adventure response (new behavior):

Situation	Adversity response/ Consequence	Adventure response/ Consequence
Big project at work, school, or home (report, term paper, house cleaning).	"I will get started tomorrow." Procrastination	"How much can I get done today?" Make it a challenge/ Increased productivity
Corporate downsizing or unexpected layoff	"I'm ruined." External control/Victim mode	"What's next?" Internal control/Reinvent oneself
Poor field conditions in sport or performing conditions for audition in the performing arts	"This is not fair." Unfocused/Shoddy performance	"Let the conditions bother the opposition and I will have an edge." Accept conditions as a given/ Solid performance

Stretch Your Performance Comfort Zone

When you discover that you are riding a dead horse, the best strategy is to dismount.

—Dakota tribal saying

The performance mind-set is not a shortcut; it is a commitment to a new way of performing in your life. Being in the performance mind-set means changing old habits and replacing them with more effective habits. These changes in thinking, feeling, and behaving can be uncomfortable and threatening. However, exceptional performance is about stretching your comfort zone. In making these changes, it is important to remember that it is okay to feel uncomfortable. Learn to be comfortable with feeling uncomfortable. Accepting that change is uncomfortable is the first step to incorporating the 5 Cs. The second step is to be patient until the new habits become a lifestyle. Although the change required to stretch your performance can be frightening, it can also be as simple as choosing to make a different sandwich.

I Make My Own Sandwiches

Sam worked on a construction site, and when the whistle blew, he would join all the other workers for lunch. Each day, Sam would open his lunch pail and complain.

"Man!" he'd shout, "Not peanut butter and jelly sandwiches again. I absolutely hate peanut butter and jelly sandwiches!"

Sam complained and whined about his peanut butter and jelly sandwiches. After many weeks of this passed, all of his co-workers became annoyed by his behavior. Finally, another member of the crew said, "Sam, if you hate peanut butter and jelly sandwiches so much, why haven't you just told your old lady to make you something different for lunch?"

"What do you mean my old lady?" Sam replied, "I'm not married. I make my own sandwiches."

—Author unknown

Put a River behind You

You have to walk the Path like a man whose head is on fire looking for water.

—Zen saying

In *The Art of War*, Sun Tzu presented the story of how Han Hsin and his army defeated the Chao State. Han Hsin's army was expected to crumble under the might of the Chao State because of the Chao State's superior numbers. Knowing that defeat was imminent, he devised a unique plan that required his entire army to make a complete and utter commitment. He placed his army so that there was a river behind them. Then he ordered them to burn all of the boats and smash their cooking pots. Han Hsin had thus placed his men in "death ground." By doing this if his men retreated they would drown and if they stayed put they would starve to death. Their only option for survival was to defeat the Chao State. This is an example of the power of real commitment as they were victorious in the face of seemingly overwhelming odds.

Experiential Activity #15:

Using the story of Han Hsin's army, identify the battles in your life that you need to win in order to support your dreams. The only way for you to win your toughest battles is to put a river behind you so that you will be inspired towards real commitment when the odds are against you. Identify an object that is symbolic of your commitment. Create a physical representation of this object so you can see or feel the object. Use this object as a positive reminder whenever your commitment is challenged or things get tough. For example, find a picture of a river (or smashed pots, burned boats) in a magazine. Cut out the picture and laminate it. Place the picture where it can be seen everyday.

Mind Gym #6: Commitment

Begin by closing your eyes and turning your attention to your breathing. Take some slow, deep breaths. Feel all of the tension leaving your body. Continue to breathe deeply in this manner for a few minutes.

Imagine that you have entered your mind gym. You are ready to increase your commitment. On the table is a DVD labeled, "Commitment." Now put this DVD into the player. As you press play, notice that the video begins with a recent situation in which you had a low level of commitment. Perhaps you skipped your workout or dragged your feet on a project. Maybe you went through the motions rather than stepping up your performance. The video is in black and white. Notice the subtitles at the bottom of the screen. What are you telling yourself to stop yourself from being exceptional?

Rewind the performance. This time you are totally committed. Your performance is now in color. Make the image brighter, turn up the volume, and bring the scene closer. Watch the same situation the way you wanted it to happen. Notice the subtitles at the bottom of the screen. What are you saying to yourself now?

Now picture your ideal day. Create your ultimate scenario. Involve all of your senses (see it, feel it, hear it, taste it, smell it). Notice as many details as possible. View yourself from an internal perspective, so that you are in your body and viewing the day through your own eyes. Make it feel as if you are living it right now. All of the commitment techniques are at your disposal. Spend several minutes carrying out your day with pure commitment. You are following through with all of your plans.

Spend several minutes experiencing your ideal day. When finished, slowly begin to open your eyes, sit quietly for a few minutes, and then orient yourself to your surroundings.

Self-reflection:
Am I committed or coasting?

Step-by-step review of developing commitment:

Step 1—

Inc. yourself

Step 2—

Make time for regeneration

Step 3—

Put a river behind you

Afterword

Before I had studied Zen for thirty years, I saw mountains as mountains and waters as waters. When I arrived at a more intimate knowledge, I came to the point where I saw that mountains are not mountains, and waters are not waters. But now that I have got its very substance I am at rest. For it's just that I see mountains once again as mountains and waters once again as waters.

—Author unknown

AFTERWORD

Do not believe anything just because a Buddha told you, but check every-thing for yourself. See if the teachings fit with your experience and be your own guiding light.

—Buddha

Do well what you dislike and the rest will be easy. Along with successes, col-lect a proper number of failures.

—Milton Erickson

The performance mind-set will help you to excel during everyday challenges and in the heat of competition. It will help you to master change and bounce back from disappointment. It will also help you to sustain high energy and main-tain good health. By participating in the activities in this book, you have a taken a gigantic step toward developing this mind-set. The mental tools and strategies in this book have been designed to assist you in becoming a more successful per-former. However, these tools are not magic. They will not make you an excep-tional performer in one day. Continue to practice the mental tools presented in this book to make them automatic in each challenge you meet.

Bibliography and Selected Sources

Bandura, Albert. *Social Learning Theory* (Prentice Hall: 1 edition, 1976).

Crews, Debbie. Putting Under Stress. *Golf Magazine* (March, 2001).

Duda, J.L. (1993). Goals: A social-cognitive approach to the study of achievement motivation in sport. In R.N. Singer, M. Murphey, & L.K. Tennant (Eds.), *Handbook of research on sport psychology* (pp. 421–436). New York: Macmillan.

Eliot, John. *Overachievement: The new model for exceptional performance* (Portfolio, 2004).

Feltz, D.L., & Landers, D.M. (1983). The effects of mental practice on motor skill learning and performance: A meta-analysis. *Journal of Sport Psychology*, 5, 25–57.

Hyams, Joe. *Zen in the Martial Arts* (Bantam: Reissue edition, 1982).

Lansing, Alfred. *Endurance: Shackelton's incredible voyage* (Carroll & Graf: 2nd edition, 1999).

Lovell, Jim. *Apollo 13: Lost Moon* (Pocket: Reissue edition, 1995).

Orlick, T., & Partington, J. (1988). Mental links to excellence. *The Sport Psychologist*, 2, 105–130.

Tzu, Sun. *The Art of War* (Oxford University Press: New Ed edition, 1971, Translated by Samuel B. Griffith), p. 86.

Weihenmayer, Erik. *Touch the Top of the World: A Blind Man's Journey to Climb Farther than the Eye Can See: My Story* (Plume: Reissue edition, 2002).

Weinberg, R.S., & Gould, D. *Foundations of Sport and Exercise Psychology.* (Human Kinetics: Second edition, 1999).

About the Author

Dr. Jim Afremow has a doctorate in sport psychology and a master's degree in counseling, both from Michigan State University. He is an Arizona Board of Behavioral Health licensed professional counselor (LPC). He has worked closely with many exceptional performers in business, sports, and the performing arts. In sports, he has consulted with collegiate, professional, and Olympic athletes. He has worked with athletes from the NFL, NHL, NBA, WNBA, MLB, PGA, and LPGA Tours. He served as the sport psychology consultant for the 2004 Greek Olympic softball team and India's 2004 Olympic field hockey team. He is employed at Arizona State University in the sports medicine department for counseling and applied sport psychology consultation. He is the sport psychology consultant at Athletes' Performance in Tempe, Arizona. He consults with individuals, couples, and families at Children and Adult Psychological Services (CAPS) in Chandler, Arizona. Dr. Afremow, and his wife, Anne, live in Ahwatukee, Arizona. Dr. Afremow can be reached through his Web site at www.lengthenyourline.com

Index

978-0-595-36318-(
0-595-36318-0

CPSIA information can be obtained at www.ICGtesting.com
Printed in the USA
LVOW06s1934240214

374971LV00001B/416/A